When the Earth

When the Earth

Lisa Young

QUATTRO BOOKS

The publication of *When the Earth* has been generously supported by the Canada Council for the Arts and the Ontario Arts Council.

Some of these poems were previously published in *Jones Av.* and *Misunderstandings Magazine*.

Cover design: Diane Mascherin
Cover photo: Hervé Barrière
Author's Photograph: Mike Lummis
Editor: Allan Briesmaster
Typography: Grey Wolf Typography

Library and Archives Canada Cataloguing in Publication

Young, Lisa
    When the earth / Lisa Young.

Poems.
Issued also in electronic format.
ISBN 978-1-926802-63-3

    I. Title.

PS8647.O626W54 2011   C811'.6   C2011-903996-6

Published by Quattro Books Inc.
89 Pinewood Avenue
Toronto, Ontario, M6C 2V2

Printed in Canada

For my parents, David and Sandra Young

Contents

When the Earth

How the Dark Early Morning Turns to Light

Slide Down On a Slew of Stars

In Childhood

Raindrops taste like gumdrops.

Forget-me-nots somersault
on your blue dress.

Buildings and houses
shrink down to crumbs
in your breadbox.

You sing to the closest
point of light in the sky,
night after night,

until she's gone,
replaced by another.

You slide down
on a slew of stars,
fear still unknown to you.

Mint

My mother lets the mint go wild
under the living room window,
in the backyard under the peach tree,
and in the garden by the rhubarb.

All of her creations
we pluck off the vine,
zucchini, cucumbers, tomatoes.

In my mother's system of green
there are stages when there is nothing to eat,
just tiny yellow-orange blossoms
and the spaces in between
where we step.

She learned from her father
how he understood the earth,
how to live by growing.

City Living

At the apartment building
just past the school
where the sun sets.

Kai stands on the cement path
where we meet.
He lives high up in the sky.

His long eyelashes curl,
his bright face
some kind of offering
to my small world.

Garden Variety

White and pink roses by the shed,
at the end of the garden,
tangled against the windows.

I pull back overgrown branches
to be with the blossoms.
Breathe them. Breathe pink, breathe white.

My paternal grandmother's voice within me:
"Not every child's born a rose."

The snapdragons hang over the cement path.
My fingers are so small,
I become their jaws and snap, snap, snap.

Snap purple and white, yellow and white
and popcorn pink.

In My Brother's Room

In my brother's room,
blue-green walls, a glade,

or an underworld
where seaweed never tangled.

Crumbling caverns
of books,

a turtle with a felt shell,
a stone in the shape of a man.

Behind the door,
a chemistry set.

In the days before we grew out
of our rooms and stopped,

we drew figure eights overlapping each other
and coloured the new shapes in.

Flight

I flew down the banister,
     ran up the kitchen stairs,
then down the front stairs.

Raced in and out of doors,
     round and round,
my dog Susie biting at my heels.

Until I flew past the purple
     velvet curtain,
the shoes, the boots, the coats,

out the front door and uphill,
     across water,
over a bridge,
     under an underpass

and no one believed me,
     even as I lifted up again,
changed course
     and headed for the inner city
in search of myself,
     someone I used to know.

Mother and Child

Clouds pass by so silently,
we're surprised when they're gone –
as if they left without
our permission.

                    This is us,
two silhouettes coming in
and out of being,
a bygone sky that keeps
slipping into now.

Today is so long ago.
You in green
and I in raucous red,
stretching under the apple tree,

all our sprawling days
beyond us.

Rock Garden

In my mother's garden,
I'm always being born in 1967.

I sit on a rock, picking up the flat stones
that can be lifted by small hands.

A tree, a star, a tune, a sigh.
Recurring dreams of waking.

The worm leaving its indent as it goes.
The quick crawl of an earwig.

Finding ants with bodies like black grapes
to tickle my hands.

Thinking of God and the way
the universe is wound around me.

Nikki & Lisa

We believed in keeping our mouths shut.

We sat on the roof and told ourselves
we weren't destined for any kind of future.

We collected fungus that grew
like mountain plateaus from the trees.

We weren't extensions of our families.
Only we existed.

We broke the piñata and dove for hard candies.
Your favourite was lime green.
I didn't know what I liked.

You never laughed loudly, laughed into
your cupped hand.

And you were happier.

I ate the moon, you swallowed the sun
and together we lived long.

Alice and Baby

Sometimes when she peeks in,
baby is there and sometimes he isn't.

Sometimes there's just a plastic bald doll,
that is all.

A mother that doesn't exist
loves a child that doesn't exist.

Alice never had a man
so who's the father of baby?

She serves rice and tea for dinner.

When baby plays mother
there is no father or child.

Alice climbs into the carriage and
that is all.

On the Way Down

Skipping along the attic hall
in orange blossom light.

The sheer stairway
grooved with black rubber treads
to make sure you don't slip.

At the top of the stair
with a bucket, cleaning each step –
listening to Gordon Lightfoot.

Was it Spring cleaning?
Where were you?
I must have been young.

It was before university –
before falling in love –
because the song was so simple

and the water warm
and not much else
to confuse things.

Don Valley

Fall leads us downward.

A nearby ravine attracts
with its steep descent,
its haunted landscape furnished
with an old train station
and the polluted river.

We pluck tart sumach,
tear the tops off reeds,
lose our way
and find ourselves
at home again.

In this hollow home,
I feel a hideous thing
tie itself to me.

Though I can't see it,
I'm on the lookout for days,
face against the screen door,
fingertips pressing on
the wire grids.

Trapped in the memory
of warmer times.

Our backyard is occupied
by stalks of plants
draped in rotting robes.

The ivy still thrives
with watercolours of green,
but the maroon stems are pervasive
and perverse.

How Do Bowls Sing?

He unpacks three brass bowls from a box
and three wooden sticks.

This is the sound the body makes
and he hits the first bowl once.

This is the sound of your heart opening
and he strikes the second bowl.

He steps down from the platform
and travels the room – around
our tables and chairs.

Then he sounds the third bowl.
This is the song of your intellect.

Our night's festivities of wine
and fiction take on a new hue.

He recounts a story about a woman
and her wish not to die alone.

You're not alone,
and he places his hand in hers.

Circling the room he walks again –
which bowl sings I can't say.

He asks us to close our eyes and see
the face of someone who has passed away.

Tell them you love them.

I see my grandmother.
She comes to my mother and me.

Nan is looking for
the white crocheted bedspread she made.

The three of us search every closet,
turn on every light, illuminate
the darkest corners.

My grandmother is crying.
She puts her arm around my shoulder and tells me:
You are the one who will find it.

When You Do Grow Up
After Lisa Jarnot

When you do grow up,
nothing will solidify.

You'll run along the river,
jump in, climb out,

become the rain,
the gush of water round a rock,
your tired legs on the run again.

You'll figure out you're a boiling pot
and what ingredients make up a day.
Everything tossed in
and dragged out of you.

You'll latch onto a slippery bank
with fine roots at work there,

and kid yourself
that you can haul ass,
beat the rapids, the falls,
the concussion.

You'll try to stay in one piece,
your tired legs on the run again,
in search of the sea.

I Am Made Of

I am made of my mother's work.

She is in my bones, urging me to
while away the afternoon,
forget the world, turn from what tires me:
the city, the refuse, the rat-infested streets.

I take my rest at the fall of water,
climb fences to forbidden places,
look up at the sky, the scattering of blue,
the riot of light.

She taught me to be my own guide.
I stay up late and keep the morning.

I am made of the bread my mother baked.
The burnt sweet I stole
before she threw the rest away.

My mother lives in me,
in the lilacs she planted in the garden.

Our souls fashioned in likeness,
I am made of my mother's work.

Bread Is Forgiving

Bread

Rye sprouts grown
in the dark,
knitting their roots together.

Wooden scoop
to scoop the flour with,
good to hold in your hand.

Carbon steel knife,
a hundred years old,
to cut hard sourdough.

You bake bread all night
while you sleep.
Feed jars of yeast starters
in the morning.

It's hard to keep track
of how bread
is always being fed
by you.

Bread, you say, is forgiving.

Daily Return

In the dirty water of wish,
I wash the dishes,
the pool in the sink rising.

Time flows free from the mind's
clogged intersection.

The skeletal feet of instinct
shift to resist a daydream,
forks, knives, spoons
gripped in rinsing.

Getting done what can be done
in the time it takes to hear
tomorrow.

Water runs off round edges,
spills a lilting sound,
the temperate song of effort
suspending the day
like a streamer in the sky.

In the dirty water of wish,
I wash the dishes,
the pool in the sink rising.

Mix Flour

I was mixing flour, sugar and salt
when the bride was pushed.
Heating butter with milk to lukewarm
when the earth blushed.

I dissolved yeast in milk and added it
to the flour mixture as she fell
into silent waters.

I kneaded well
as she passed the icebergs that run deep.

I covered and set two hours
while the dough rose,
thinking of the golden kiss of the groom.
Then I cut him into pieces,
three inches in diameter.

He shoved her off the totem pole
and I draped a damp cloth over him.
Allowed the dough to rise for thirty minutes.
A low man, all tongue.

I placed him on a pan in a slow oven.
Let him cool by the kitchen window.
This afternoon,
dipped him in syrup.

Sweeping

After dinner, you sweep
across the kitchen.

Behind the fridge find
new territory,
a dividing wall
you've never leaned on.

You travel in a circle,
stop by the window,
kneel down and sweep under
the hutch with your broom.

As slow and awkward as
stirring a bowl of dough,
you attend to the task.

You become
what you collect, a dispersion of dust,
cheek against the floor.

Farmer's Fare

Edible flowers
or fresh figs for a salad.

Kumquats with bodies like tiny oval
oranges and insides like lemons.

Shredded basil for squares of pasta.

Harvested potatoes baked
and topped with homemade sour cream.

In the herb garden,
I cut handfuls of chives.

The wild green hair
leaves their scent
on fingers and thumbs.

Blossoms as round as dandelions
turning to seed.

Purple petal-like tepals
lean into the sun,
witness another way of being.

I pluck out each tepal like a tooth
and count them one by one.

Householder

My house is overrun by a woman.

I discovered her last Wednesday,
her profile reflected in the mirror
behind the bathroom door.

She was desperate, the dark dream
of my unseemly self.

I found the back room
strewn with a thousand articles
that weren't mine:

Piles of clothes I'd never seen before
and plates filled with
scraps of meat and bones
littered on the floor.

In the walls, down the halls
her long skirt trails.

Hide and go seek. She's in
the grain of this house.

On the Way

Outside one of those rural superstores,
young boys scale sacks of black earth.

What else are they climbing on?
Red soil, woodchips?
I can't make out the signs.

While I linger,
my other half grabs what we need.

Our list is meager, just a bottle
of wine and a basket of berries,
but the getting of them is eternal.

In this remote place on high ground,
other realities call out.

The horizon tries to tell me
about time and how long it will last.

Ahead, an elderly man
carries a bag of milk
by the scruff of its neck.

He's heroic as he struggles
with the necessary goods.

I just stand here and wait.

The heat of the parking lot
rises through my soles,
the sun hisses at cars.

From a field far off
a rooster crows.
It sounds like he's saying,
"Behold."

The Craft of Jewellery Making

The design eludes me
        and I begin again.

Imitations of symmetry born
        on a July afternoon
too close for clothes,
        my youngest sprinting
round the house.

My centre stone's encumbered.
        Outlying beads dangle
at odd angles
        and slide dangerously
next to the core.

In between getting it wrong
        and getting it all right,
I attach the clasps.

When the Earth

When the Earth

When the earth is a bowl,
      the sky will widen.
I only want a hill to sit on.

Tonight pines gather
      and lean into forest's centre,
their hunched backs
      a new impression.
What do they protect?

Coyote's yowl through the fields
      is a part of me.

Even the darkness has changed.
      It breathes me in.

I fly across the muck of a pond's edge,
      dip into midnight
where the top of the sky
      holds me
in an age long past.

Pond

The pond reflects
the heart muscle,
its pathways, its work.

The quiet surface holds
untold organisms, parts,
plots and ponderings.

Glide in – trespass –
dive deep and find
what never planned on being found.

The bass will bite your shoulder.
You are something good
to eat.

In a splash
of fear, it's impossible
to keep still.

Put the pond behind you, then.
Reach for a cold wrought iron seat
and dry yourself in silence.

Hyacinth

Hyacinth is a cultivated lily.
      Her husks rub and split
like the shucking of
      so much corn.

Roots set,
      plum fingertips furled,
she waits for colour,
      newborn eyes.

The arrival –
      a letting down,
an accumulation of weight
      into wilt.

In Praise of Underneath
After Gregory Orr

Around the foxgloves we weed
wiry new growth
impossible
to rip apart

and yet we try,
twisting a stub
of stem, bright green
at its centre.

The natural shapes
long
for our attention.

Earth all the while craving
to be turned over
and over again.

We're craving too.

We don't love the bloom enough.

Under the fullness
of magnolia canopy,
who can guess at death?

In the open lane in back,
a red fox rips into
a tender shadow.

Pond Dreams

The polluted pond with its jagged steel and crushed glass.
      Bullfrogs send out their calls.
Listen to me.

The pond dreamed again.
      A white column lodged at its centre.
I talk of the pond,
      saying, I've dreamed of this.
The old woman who owns the water says, Hush.
      Her face never changes over the years.

In a room overlooking the pond,
      a girl prepares to go out. Mirror fragments
on the floor. By her bed, bulrushes
      and a manmade disaster: a drain
that won't let itself be seen.

The pond dreams of turtle-woman.
      Her human self emerges, covered
in moss and water lilies. Her shell
      becomes a hat.

She floats on her back, looking up at the sky.
      In the forest beyond,
black-capped chickadees sing
      yoo hoo, yoo hoo,
above and out of my dreams.

Algonquin

The bow matters today.

Cowlick branches
in the face of the river.

Fallen trees,
a spooning couple in a fire of green,
reach across the dunes.

A falcon haunts the sky,
the sunshine as sweet as liqueur.

June has lifted the nadir
to above ground level, in this

your first summer as a father.

Nerves shellacked by a new day,
cracks in the oar appear
as a part of the design.

Rivulets sketch moss-green glass
and bubbly white crystal.

Bourbon, too strong for the morning,
your coolant for the portages.

Your daughter's echo, a call
to remember this aging landscape.

Rain Walk

The rain's so polite I can barely hear her.

I wander past the old wooden steps,
mint leaves growing out from under.

The maple tree is losing her bark,
her years shortening.

The rain's picking up by the river.

Weigela bells cluster in bliss
near the evergreens.

In the ash tree, dead branches tangle,
tenderly held up for passersby.

I stand where the wild reeds grow,
the red raft moored to the shore.

I hear her now.

"Come," says the rain, "come hither."

Cherry Tree

To find the cherry tree,
don't do
what everyone else is doing.

Ask yourself how to be,
be any old thing as you wander.

Wander past the mulberry tree
where the flies race and circle
round the fallen berries.

Discover the white roses.
        Then you see the bridge
you didn't see before.

It's made of old wood,
not more than a few steps long,
with a rise in the middle.

A lantern marks this bridge.

On the other side,
the cherry tree will appear,
a sight you've never tasted before.

Ask her anything.
Ask her how to be.

What the Trees Say

Maple, with boughs as high as a ballroom ceiling, says,
Dance under me.

Elm, with many arms moving like Saraswati, says,
Grow, grow.

Quiet ash, way in the distance, says,
Look inward.

Willow, with leaves skirting the ground, says,
Shh, I'm sleeping.

Oak, with dead branches hanging down, says,
Look above. I still carry leaves to awaken you.

Jack Pine, reaching with outstretched arms, says,
Breathe another reality.

Downward

Apples and pears will fall and fall
if no one takes them for their own.

We follow the season down and down,
under and under.

How do you follow, leading the way?
You see who people are as they
bend into new territory.

How letting go,
instead of holding on,
becomes the aim.

Fall might now be a change
you embrace.

The blue sky has taken over
without our noticing.

Breathe bits of blue.

How do you love blue
when it's everywhere?

The rake set against a tree in the grove,
an invitation:

begin collecting summer's end.

Evergreens

You might think evergreens
love the Fall,
smug in their greenness
while neighbours turn
yellow to orange to hanging on
for dear-life red.

Evergreens become greener
and greener; envy the letting go
of the maple leaves,
the vivid movement around them.

Carapace

I choose what doesn't matter,
           swinging from swing to swing.
Branches and bristles swish and whip,
           sun against me
giving its unholy hot attention.

Muck, stone, water,
           the next step's sharp edge.
Every sensation pushed forward
           where no part of the forest
wants me to go.

I tread on the swamp's chest,
           fall into myself,
into a lake.

On an island rock,
           I follow the slow gift of the turtle
who takes a long time to swim
           right past me.

Here words are soon forgotten
           in the silence,
in the subtle movement of the turtle's legs.

The way he floats by,
           untouchable, free
and yet more mine
           than anything I own.

Field and Sky

The moon was so bright. What to make of it?
You kept to the stars,
the tiniest twinkling star until it stopped.

How that field and sky feel like home.

When someone you don't expect
comes along in the night
and asks what part of the sky you love best,
you're startled.

How looking up at that small star
reminded you of yourself,
when the world was the future
and you had no idea of the mystery.

And yet, you're still here.
The gate is wide open,
all day, every day.
No place you can't wander.

The jewelweed, bright orange lights,
line the path,
frogs jump among the reeds.

Take your chair right down by the edge
and watch the fish in the shallows.

The divine madness of pond life
threatened by those reeds,
a swamp in the making.

The milkweed pods so tempting
to pull apart.

Up the hill, you pass by yourself,
look back and keep walking,
toward the field that calls the sky
or down to the house for company and coffee.

How the Dark Early Morning Turns to Light

Opening

Anything can become a surprise.
How the dark early morning turns to light.

How your own kind of awkwardness
is a question.

Snow so slight it takes a moment to notice.
Fine dust falling from the sky as if

clouds are coffee tables in need
of being wiped clean.

Light that glides into the room
and lands on your desk,

its rays lifting a rainbow off
an almost empty glass.

Movements

In summer
the barn is cold in the mornings,
coldest by the windows
where I stand.

We take our place
for the east-west dance,
a practice of backward steps,

a swaying on one foot
now another,
arms sculpting the air
in opposition

until the complaints crowding
this breaking day are displaced
by the call of the piano
and the movements

leading us to see
we are arms and legs,
we come with a body.

Observatory

Before the empty
bookcase of night,
hunger beads round our necks.

We aren't the same,
therefore we have a lot
in common.

We lock arms, flatten
our hearts,
rarely meet in the middle.

The silly music of our souls
tastes a distant melody,
licks the twist of sound.

We could go another way,
after the pepper mill,
into the Virginia reel.

Climb the octaves in the garden.
Calendula growing over
would-be graves.

Leave behind the trowel,
our feather skin and long bones
good at playing dead.

Stop come midnight,
our bodies smouldering
under new stars.

The Way of Yellow

Once, a bit of sun crept into my closet
        and stayed there –
food for the moths.

I never chose yellow,
        not for a flower or a shirt or a balloon.

I chose orange,
        lived my orange-walled life
and dreamt of throwing oranges
        over castle walls

to fight the enemy – the enemy was you –
        the oranges a kind of offering.

I never chose yellow,
        not for anything.

How to learn to love the colour of yolk?

And yet, papaya and mango both turn yellowy.
        I could turn
to yellow.

What I See

The canopy of maple tree waves
       high above the roof of the house.
Shadow of a door flung open.

My father in repose.
       An ancient pear tree waiting
to be noticed.

My father raises his glass in thirst
       and contemplation.
A curled brown leaf becomes a canoe,
       glides across the grass.

My father's distant look,
       where ideas formulate.
Clouds hold court with the skies.

My father takes another sip –
       head up and then down.
Silhouette of leaves quilting the ground.

And my father is gone.
       The inner door closes
behind him.

Cedar

I love the curl of wood
a plane offers up.

The coiled stories emerging,
falling to the ground
in a generous array.

Sawdust is loveable too
and loves,
covering every surface
of a room.

Once I sanded a door until
sawdust changed the landscape.

In Praise of Work, 1
After P.K. Page

Her clothes on the line stiffen and buckle,
the fringe of a blue shawl the only part free
to tremble like high notes on a piano.

In the graveyard beyond, tree branches
are sewn into the clouds,
headstones come alive, the people forgotten.

She washes the distance down to the ground.
Soaks, presses and dries the linen skies,
looking neither up nor all around.

The bedposts of the trees are dusted and polished,
rivers shaken out like welcome mats,
undulations of the sea shined like carved wood.

Halos of the sun and moon pondered,
the cirrus clouds swirled in a suds-filled basin,
rinsed and combed with hands that are careful.

Everything, outside and in, given room
to float up or drop like an anchor,
the swaying trees keeping time.

Relic Spinning Wheel

Ancient spinner,
spin the bag of wool.

Push the pedal,
spin the wheel, until

you abandon wool
and work with air.

Too thin,
the snap of what is.

A discolouration of effort
as the spindle fills.

Elusive material tricks
your fingers.

The atmosphere
undulates, entwines.

Let yourself be spun.

In Praise of Work, 2
After P.K. Page

In the windowed attic,
her marionette strings attach beyond
to the clouds and stars.

Her instruments the bucket, the rag,
the dusty wooden floor,
a drawer in a night table.

Each inner corner thought of,
caressed, her fist
squeezing the cloth in the air.

The atmosphere cleaned
by her creased fingers,
the praiseful hands that see.

Lantern

Dangling, bridging, lighting the lane,
finely glittering in the present,
a lantern is mothering.

She swings westward,
rhythmically finds the greys and the greens.

The secret road behind the houses
where bunnies are born.

A garage, a magic hat
bursting with running rabbits, wire cages open.

The movement of birth, of ever-expanding life,
hopping down the cracked pavement,
a multitude of desires.

She searches out passersby.
Invites all to her vigil.

Come alone, she says. Be alone
in the rising crowd.

The Bell

She pulls the string of the bell.

The bell outside the summer kitchen.
It's fall.

Fall in all its mourning colours.

Colours of grey, maroon and beige.
The beige of a crusted flower.

A flower that has no light, or a thistle.
Thistle ball that crumples.

Crumples in her hands, laced in dryness.
Dryness of the season,

a season where dead houseflies collect on radiators.
Radiators that overheat or don't work at all.

All the stars so clear, she can see their shapes.
Like the shapes of the forest, each bare tree a shock.

A shock to see the trees without their clothes.
Without clothes, they are silent.

In silence, she's nearer, not farther away from herself,
her self easily lost in the greys.

In the Dressing Room

i.

To remember is to be confused.
To remember is to slip
into a high-up – too high – world.

I trace the blurred edges
of the locked door,
last night's dream in my pocket.

The apple's inside Eve.
It's the centre of her pleasure
and I crumple to the carpet.
I need the ground to hold on to.

Venus hangs above the pond.
She's calling me up.
The blue pattern is not solid.
It ripples.
I am both here and there.

ii.

In the summer of dreams,
I live in this deep winter,
a season where I collect beads,
green pearls that turn to sweet peas
my mother planted every year.

I recall the sun,
trade sweaters for sleeveless camisoles
as venous ice forms along the ceiling.

iii.

He comes as a winter God,
a blue jay of blue ice.
He's king. Invites me into a snow cave.

I resolve no longer to write my dreams –
to remember.
I lose the blue notebook with the face
of a hungry moon.

iv.

To dream is to cheat, to steal what isn't mine.
I need to return to all that failed.
It's who I am.

I leave everything I try on
in the dressing room.
The mirror stays with me.

As I travel Queen Street, inside the bus,
I see no one.

Glimpse

The leaves are up and flying.
At the stove, in pink shorts,
my partner's distraught over a dirty pan.

How do I hold each day?

Loop round the warp, throw
the shuttle, exchange the heddles,
tighten the weft.

I still yearn for that blue breeze with a dash
of daisies,
bay windows open to the tops of trees.

Which days can I hold?

Warehouse casements surround,
I'm on tiptoe to find the right colour
among all the skeins of wool for the loom.

Way at the back, at the top,
I choose magenta.

The East End is still my ethereal archive.
Ghostly imprints replay a thousand days.

The sound of the train is not as empty
or as sad here.
Branches reflect in the panes across the street.
Dust in the eyes.

I map and then lapse into
the sky of my old neighbourhood
where the leaves glitter in the sun
like waves on a lake's surface.

I breathe in the light before
the thunder rolls and the leaves fly.

Everything Counts

Everything counts.
This red streetcar moving me forward.
This movement of swaying.

The driver I can't see and the early day
I can't quite grasp as we all ride together
to our destinations.

Out of the stupor, the grand grey buildings
mar the horizon.
Under everything, everything counts.

Under everything that tenses,
spoils, tricks, loses, angers
is something else –
hibernating beneath the melting snow,
in the dense layers of doom.

Underneath, in the spine, is the wish
to embrace this existence – whatever
it might be – the blue ink, the letters,
the words, the stories forming.

¤

In the breath is the wish.
In the chest is the wish.
In the bones of the feet.

In the black forest.
In the sea, near the shore.
In the recline of a lawn chair, face to the sun.

In the paper shuffle is the wish.
In the stillness of pondering.
In the bird's echo.

In the imprint left by house guests
who all leave at once.
In the tulips that bloom on your kitchen table.

In the red exit sign is the wish.
In the German Shepherd's eager paws.
In the moan of the snow plough.
In the coffin lowering into the grave
is the wish.

¤

Everything counts.

Just to remember is enough.
Just to be here is enough.
To have this morning enough.
This glass of water enough.
This deep breath
is enough.

Acknowledgements

Allan Briesmaster for his sagacity.
John Calabro for his superpowers.
Luciano Iacobelli for his insight.
Beatriz Hausner for her humour.
Maddy Curry for her care.
Kate Sorbara for her guidance.
Martha Heyneman for her teaching.
Craig Proctor for his direction.
Michael Fraser for his shepherding.
David Clink for his understanding.
The writers in my writing groups
for their inspiration.
Sandra Kasturi for her leadership.
Stuart Ross for his wisdom.
Sonia Di Placido for her perception.
Iza Bryniarska for her generosity.
Andrea Ledwell for her loyalty.
Rod Weatherbie for his ear.
Johanne Pulker for her friendship.
Lindsay Smail for her poetry.
Mark Young for his enthusiasm.
Mike Lummis for his openness.

Other Quattro Poetry Books